The Constitution of
The State of Kansas:
A Quick Reference Guide

Bootblack Budget Books
Copyright 2018 ©
ISBN-13: 978-1985311282
ISBN-10: 1985311283

Contents:

Ordinances – Page 23

Section 1. School Sections

Section 2. University Lands

Section 3. Lands for Public Buildings

Section 4. Lands for Benevolent Institutions

Section 5. Salt Springs and Mines

Section 6. Proceeds to Schools

Section 7. School Lands

Section 8. Selection of Lands

Preamble – 25

Kansas Bill of Rights – Page 26

Section 1. Equal Rights

Section 2. Political Power; Privileges

Section 3. Right of Peaceable Assembly; Petition

Section 4. Individual Right to Bear Arms; Armies

Section 5. Trial By Jury

Section 6. Slavery Prohibited; Servitude for Conviction of a Crime

Section 7. Religious Liberty Property Qualification for Public Office

Section 8. Habeas Corpus

Section 9. Bail; Fines; Cruel And Unusual Punishment

Section 10. Trial; Defense of Accused; Witness Against Self; Double Jeopardy.

Section 11. Liberty Of Press and Speech; Libel

Section 12. No Forfeiture of Estate for Crimes

Section 13. Treason

Section 14. Soldiers Quarters

Section 15. Search and Seizure

Section 16. Imprisonment for Debt

Section 17. Property Rights of Citizens and Aliens

Section 18. Justice Without Delay

Section 19. Emoluments or Privileges Prohibited

Section 20. Powers Retained by People

Section 21. Right of the Public to Hunt, Fish, and Trap Wildlife

Article I: Executive – Page 30

Section 1. Executive Officers; Selection; Terms

Section 2. Eliminated by revision.

Section 3. Executive Power of Governor

Section 4. Reports to Governor

Section 5. Governor's Duties for Legislature; Messages; Special Sessions; Adjournment

Section 6. Reorganization of State Agencies of Executive Branch

Section 7. Pardons

Section 8. Eliminated by revision.

Section 9. State seal and Commissions

Section 10. Eliminated by revision.

Section 11. Vacancies in Executive Offices

Section 12. Lieutenant Governor

Section 13. Eliminated by revision.

Section 14. Eliminated by revision.

Section 15. Compensation of Officers

Section 16. Eliminated by revision.

Article II: Legislative – Page 35

Section 1. Legislative Power

Section 2. Senators and Representatives

Section 3. Compensation of Members of Legislature

Section 4. Qualifications of Members

Section 5. Eligibility and Disqualification of Members

Section 6. Eliminated by revision.

Section 7. Eliminated by revision.

Section 8. Organization and Sessions

Section 9. Vacancies in Legislature

Section 10. Journals

Section 11. Eliminated by revision.

Section 12. Origination by Either house

Section 13. Majority for Passage of Bills

Section 14. Approval of Bills; Vetoes

Section 15. Requirements Before Bill Passed

Section 16. Subject and Title of Bills; Amendment or Revival of Statutes

Section 17. Uniform Operation of Laws of a General Nature

Section 18. Election or Appointment of Officers; Filling Vacancies

Section 19. Publication of Acts

Section 20. Enacting Clause of Bills; Laws Enacted Only by Bill

Section 21. Delegation of Powers of Local Legislation and Administration

Section 22. Legislative Immunity

Section 23. Eliminated by Revision.

Section 24. Appropriations

Section 25. Eliminated by Revision.

Section 26. Repealed.

Section 27. Impeachment

Section 28. Officers Impeachable; Grounds; Punishment

Section 29. Eliminated by Revision.

Section 30. Delegation of Powers to Interstate Bodies

Article III: Judicial – Page 42

Section 1. Judicial Power; Seals; Rules

Section 2. Supreme Court

Section 3. Jurisdiction and Terms

Section 4. Reporter; Clerk

Section 5. Selection of Justices of the Supreme Court

Section 6. District Courts

Section 7. Qualifications of Justices and Judges

Section 8. Prohibition of Political Activity by Justices and Certain Judges

Section 9. Eliminated by revision.

Section 10. Eliminated by revision.

Section 11. Stricken from article.

Section 12. Extension of Terms Until Successor Qualified

Section 13. Compensation of Justices and Judges; Certain Limitation

Section 14. Eliminated by revision.

Section 15. Removal of Justices and Judges

Section 16. Savings Clause

Section 17. Eliminated by revision.

Section 18. Stricken from article.

Section 19. Eliminated by revision.

Section 20. Eliminated by revision.

Article IV: Elections – Page 49

Section 1. Mode of Voting

Section 2. General Elections.

Section 3. Recall of Elected Officials

Section 4. Eliminated by revision.

Section 5. Eliminated by revision.

Article V: Suffrage – Page 50

Section 1. Qualifications of Electors

Section 2. Disqualification to Vote

Section 3. Eliminated by Revision

Section 4. Proof of Right to Vote

Section 5. Repealed.

Section 6. Eliminated by revision.

Section 7. Privileges of Electors

Section 8. Eliminated by revision.

Article VI: Education – Page 52

Section 1. Schools and Related Institutions and Activities

Section 2. State Board of Education and State Board of Regents

Section 3. Members of State Board of Education and State Board of Regents

Section 4. Commissioner of Education

Section 5. Local Public Schools

Section 6. Finance

Section 7. Savings Clause

Section 8. Eliminated by amendment.

Section 9. Eliminated by amendment.

Section 10. Eliminated by amendment.

Article VII: Public Institutions and Welfare – Page 56

Section 1. Benevolent Institutions

Section 2. Eliminated by revision.

Section 3. Eliminated by revision.

Section 4. Aged and Infirm Persons; Financial Aid; State Participation

Section 5. Unemployment Compensation; Old-Age Benefits; Taxation

Section 6. Tax Levy for Certain Institutions

Article VIII: Militia – Page 58

Section 1. Composition; Exemption

Section 2. Organization

Section 3. Officers

Section 4. Commander in Chief

Article IX: County and Township Organization – Page 59

Section 1. Counties

Section 3. Stricken from the constitution.

Section 4. Stricken from the constitution.

Section 5. Removal of officers

Article X: Appointment of the Legislature – Page 60

Section 1. Reapportionment of Senatorial and Representative Districts

Section 2. Eliminated by revision.

Section 3. Repealed.

Article XI: Finance and Taxation – Page 62

Section 1. System of Taxation; Classification; Exemption

Section 2. Taxation of Incomes

Section 3. Transferred and Renumbered.

Section 4. Revenue for Current Expenses

Section 5. Object of Tax

Section 6. State Debts; Annual Tax; Proceeds

Section 7. Election on Indebtedness

Section 8. Borrowing Money by State

Section 9. Internal Improvements; State Highway System; Flood Control; Conservation or Development of Water Resources

Section 10. Special Taxes for Highway Purposes

Section 11. Taxation of Incomes; Adoption of Federal Laws by Reference

Section 12. Assessment and Taxation of Land Devoted to Agricultural Use

Section 13. Exemption of Property for Economic Development Purposes; Procedure; Limitations

Article XII: Corporations – Page 70

Section 1. Corporate Powers

Section 2. Liability of stockholders

Section 3. Repealed

Section 4. Rights of Way; Eminent Domain

Section 5. Cities Powers of Home Rule

Section 6. Definition of Corporations; Suits

Article XIII: Banks – Page 74

Section 1. Banking Laws

Section 2. State not to be Stockholder

Section 3. Eliminated by revision.

Section 4. Eliminated by revision.

Section 5. Transferred and renumbered as Section 2 by revision.

Section 6. Eliminated by revision.

Section 7. Eliminated by revision.

Section 8. Eliminated by revision.

Section 9. Eliminated by revision.

Article XIV: Constitutional Amendment and Revision – Page 75

Section 1. Proposals by Legislature; Approval by Electors

Section 2. Constitutional Conventions; Approval by Electors

Article XV: Miscellaneous – Page 78

Section 1. Selection of Officers

Section 2. Tenure of Office; Merit System in Civil Service

Section 3. Lotteries

Section 3A. Regulation, Licensing and Taxation of "bingo" Games Authorized

Section 3B. Regulation, Licensing and Taxation of Horse and Dog Racing and Parimutuel Wagering Thereon

Section 3C. State-Owned and Operated Lottery

Section 3D. Regulation of "Raffles" Authorized

Section 4. Repealed.

Section 5. Financial Statements; Publication

Section 7. Salaries Reduced for Neglect of Duty

Section 8. Location of State Capital

Section 9. Homestead Exemption

Section 10. Intoxicating Liquors

Section 11. Repealed.

Section 12. Membership or Non-membership in Labor Organizations

Section 13. Continuity of State and Local Governmental Operations

Section 15. Victims Rights

Section 16. Marriage

The Constitution of The State of Kansas

Ordinance:

WHEREAS, The government of the United States is the proprietor of a large portion of the lands included in the limits of the state of Kansas as defined by this constitution; and,

WHEREAS, The state of Kansas will possess the right to tax said lands for purposes of government, and for other purposes; Now, therefore,

Be it ordained by the people of Kansas:

That the right of the state of Kansas to tax such lands is relinquished forever, and the state of Kansas will not interfere with the title of the United States to such lands, nor with any regulation of congress in relation thereto, nor tax nonresidents higher than residents: Provided always, That the following conditions be agreed to by congress:

Section 1. School Sections

Sections numbered sixteen and thirty-six in each township in the state, including Indian reservations and trust lands, shall be granted to the state for the exclusive use of common schools; and when either of said sections, or any part thereof, has been disposed of, other lands of equal value, as nearly contiguous thereto as possible, shall be substituted therefore.

Section 2. University Lands

That seventy-two sections of land shall be granted to the state for the erection and maintenance of a state university.

Section 3. Lands for public buildings

That thirty-six sections shall be granted to the state for the erection of public buildings.

Section 4. Lands for benevolent institutions

That seventy-two sections shall be granted to the state for the erection and maintenance of charitable and benevolent institutions.

Section 5. Salt springs and mines

That all salt springs, not exceeding twelve in number, with six sections of land adjacent to each, together with all mines, with the lands necessary for the full use, shall be granted to the state for works of public improvement.

Section 6. Proceeds to schools

That five percentum of the proceeds of the public lands in Kansas, disposed of after the admission of the state into the union, shall be paid to the state for a fund, the income of which shall be used for the support of common schools.

Section 7. School lands

That the five hundred thousand acres of land to which the state is entitled under the act of congress entitled "An act to appropriate the proceeds of the sales of public lands and grant pre-emption rights," approved September 4th, 1841, shall be granted to the state for the support of common schools.

Section 8. Selection of lands

That the lands hereinbefore mentioned shall be selected in such manner as may be prescribed by law; such selections to be subject to the approval of the commissioner of the general land office of the United States.

Preamble

We, the people of Kansas, grateful to Almighty God for our civil and religious privileges, in order to insure the full enjoyment of our rights as American citizens, do ordain and establish this constitution of the state of Kansas, with the following boundaries, to wit: Beginning at a point on the western boundary of the state of
Missouri, where the thirty-seventh parallel of north latitude crosses the same; thence running west on said parallel to the twenty-fifth meridian of longitude west from Washington; thence north on said meridian to the fortieth parallel of north latitude; thence east on said parallel to the western boundary of the state of Missouri; thence south with the western boundary of said state to the place of beginning.

Kansas Bill of Rights

Section 1. Equal Rights

All men are possessed of equal and inalienable natural rights, among which are life, liberty, and the pursuit of happiness.

Section 2. Political Power; Privileges

All political power is inherent in the people, and all free governments are founded on their authority, and are instituted for their equal protection and benefit. No special privileges or immunities shall ever be granted by the legislature, which may not be altered, revoked or repealed by the same body; and this power shall be exercised by no other tribunal or agency.

Section 3. Right of Peaceable Assembly; Petition

The people have the right to assemble, in a peaceable manner, to consult for their common good, to instruct their representatives, and to petition the government, or any department thereof, for the redress of grievances.

Section 4. Individual Right to Bear Arms; Armies

A person has the right to keep and bear arms for the defense of self, family, home and state, for lawful hunting and recreational use, and for any other lawful purpose; but standing armies, in time of peace, are dangerous to liberty, and shall not be tolerated, and the military shall be in strict subordination to the civil power.

Section 5. Trial By Jury

The right of trial by jury shall be inviolate.

Section 6. Slavery Prohibited; Servitude for Conviction of a Crime

There shall be no slavery in this state; and no involuntary servitude, except for the punishment of crime, whereof the party shall have been duly convicted.

Section 7. Religious Liberty Property Qualification for Public Office

The right to worship God according to the dictates of conscience shall never be infringed; nor shall any person be compelled to attend or support any form of worship; nor shall any control of or interference with the rights of conscience be permitted, nor any preference be given by law to any religious establishment or mode of worship. No religious test or property qualification shall be required for any office of public trust, nor for any vote at any elections, nor shall any person be incompetent to testify on account of religious belief.

Section 8. Habeas Corpus

The right to the writ of habeas corpus shall not be suspended, unless the public safety requires it in case of invasion or rebellion.

Section 9. Bail; Fines; Cruel And Unusual Punishment

All persons shall be bailable by sufficient sureties except for capital offenses, where proof is evident or the presumption great. Excessive bail shall not be required, nor excessive fines imposed, nor cruel or unusual punishment inflicted.

Section 10. Trial; Defense of Accused; Witness Against Self; Double Jeopardy.

In all prosecutions, the accused shall be allowed to appear and defend in person, or by counsel; to demand the nature and cause of the accusation against him; to meet the witness face to face, and to have compulsory process to compel the attendance of the witnesses in his behalf, and a speedy public trial by an impartial jury of the county or district in which the offense is alleged to have been committed. No person shall be a witness against himself, or be twice put in jeopardy for the same offense.

Section 11. Liberty Of Press and Speech; Libel

The liberty of the press shall be inviolate; and all persons may freely speak, write or publish their sentiments on all subjects, being responsible for the abuse of such rights; and in all civil or criminal actions for libel, the truth may be given in evidence to the jury, and if it shall appear that the alleged libelous matter was published for justifiable ends, the accused party shall be acquitted.

Section 12. No Forfeiture of Estate for Crimes

No conviction within the state shall work a forfeiture of estate.

Section 13. Treason

Treason shall consist only in levying war against the state, adhering to its enemies, or giving them aid and comfort. No person shall be convicted of treason unless on the evidence of two witnesses to the overt act, or confession in open court.

Section 14. Soldiers Quarters

No soldier shall, in time of peace, be quartered in any house without the consent of the occupant, nor in time of war, except as prescribed by law.

Section 15. Search and Seizure

The right of the people to be secure in their persons and property against unreasonable searches and seizures shall be inviolate; and no warrant shall issue but on probable cause, supported by oath or affirmation, particularly describing the place to be searched and the persons or property to be seized.

Section 16. Imprisonment for Debt

No person shall be imprisoned for debt, except in cases of fraud.

Section 17. Property Rights of Citizens and Aliens

No distinction shall ever be made between citizens of the state of Kansas and the citizens of other states and territories of the United States in reference to the purchase, enjoyment or descent of property. The rights of aliens in reference to the purchase, enjoyment or descent of property may be regulated by law.

Section 18. Justice Without Delay

All persons, for injuries suffered in person, reputation or property, shall have remedy by due course of law, and justice administered without delay.

Section 19. Emoluments or Privileges Prohibited

No hereditary emoluments, honors, or privileges shall ever be granted or conferred by the state.

Section 20. Powers Retained by People

This enumeration of rights shall not be construed to impair or deny others retained by the people; and all powers not herein delegated remain with the people.

Section 21. Right of the Public to Hunt, Fish, and Trap Wildlife

The people have the right to hunt, fish and trap, including by the use of traditional methods, subject to reasonable laws and regulations that promote wildlife conservation and management and that preserve the future of hunting and fishing. Public hunting and fishing shall be a preferred means of managing and controlling wildlife. This section shall not be construed to modify any provision of law relating to trespass, property rights or water resources.

Article I: Executive

Section 1. Executive Officers; Selection; Terms

The constitutional officers of the executive department shall be the governor, lieutenant governor, secretary of state, and attorney general, who shall have such qualifications as are provided by law. Such officers shall be chosen by the electors of this state at the time of voting for members of the legislature in the year 1974 and every four years thereafter, and such officers elected in 1974 and thereafter shall have terms of four years which shall begin on the second Monday of January next after their election, and until their successors are elected and qualified. In the year 1974 and thereafter, at all elections of governor and lieutenant governor the candidates for such offices shall be nominated and elected jointly in such manner as is prescribed by law so that a single vote shall be cast for a candidate for governor and a candidate for lieutenant governor running together, and if such candidates are nominated by petition or convention each petition signature and each convention vote shall be made for a candidate for governor and a candidate for lieutenant governor running together. No person may be elected to more than two successive terms as governor nor to more than two successive terms as lieutenant governor.

Section 2. Eliminated by revision.

Section 3. Executive Power of Governor

The supreme executive power of this state shall be vested in a governor, who shall be responsible for the enforcement of the laws of this state.

Section 4. Reports to Governor

The governor may require information in writing from the officers of the executive department, upon any subject relating to their respective duties. The officers of the executive department, and of all public state institutions, shall, at least ten days preceding each regular session of the legislature, severally report to the governor, who shall transmit such reports to the legislature.

Section 5. Governor's Duties for Legislature; Messages; Special Sessions; Adjournment

The governor may, on extraordinary occasions, call the legislature into special session by proclamation; and shall call the legislature into special session, upon petition signed by at least two-thirds of the members elected to each house. At every session of the legislature the governor shall communicate in writing information in reference to the condition of the state, and recommend such measures as he deems expedient. In case of disagreement between the two houses in respect of the time of adjournment, the governor may adjourn the legislature to such time as he deems proper, not beyond its next regular session.

Section 6. Reorganization of State Agencies of Executive Branch

(a) For the purpose of transferring, abolishing, consolidating or coordinating the whole or any part of any state agency, or the functions thereof, within the executive branch of state government, when the governor considers the same necessary for efficient administration, he may issue one or more executive reorganization orders, each bearing an identifying number, and transmit the same to the legislature within the first thirty calendar days of any regular session. Agencies and functions of the legislative and judicial branches, and constitutionally delegated functions of state officers and state boards shall be exempt from executive reorganization orders.

(b) The governor shall transmit each executive reorganization order to both houses of the legislature on the same day, and each such order shall be accompanied by a governor's message which shall specify with respect to each abolition of a function included in the order the statutory authority for the exercise of the function. Every executive reorganization order shall provide for the transfer or other disposition of the records, property and personnel affected by the order. Every executive reorganization order shall provide for all necessary transfers of unexpended balances of appropriations of agencies affected by such order, and such changes in responsibility for and handling of special funds as may be necessary to accomplish the purpose of such order. Transferred balances of appropriations may be used only for the purposes for which the appropriation was originally made.

(c) Each executive reorganization order transmitted to the legislature as provided in this section shall take effect and have the force of general law on the July 1 following its transmittal to the legislature, unless within sixty calendar days and before the adjournment of the legislative session either the senate or the house of representatives adopts by a majority vote of the members elected thereto a resolution disapproving such executive reorganization order. Under the provisions of an executive reorganization order a portion of the order may be effective at a time later than the date on which the order is otherwise effective.

(d) An executive reorganization order which is effective shall be published as and with the acts of the legislature and the statutes of the state. Any executive reorganization order which is or is to become effective may be amended or repealed as statutes of the state are amended or repealed.

Section 7. Pardons

The pardoning power shall be vested in the governor, under regulations and restrictions prescribed by law.

Section 8. Eliminated by revision.

Section 9. State seal and Commissions

There shall be a seal of the state, which shall be kept by the governor, and used by him officially, and which shall be the great seal of Kansas. All commissions shall be issued in the name of the state of Kansas; and shall be signed by the governor, countersigned by the secretary of state, and sealed with the great seal.

Section 10. Eliminated by revision.

Section 11. Vacancies in Executive Offices

When the office of governor is vacant, the lieutenant governor shall become governor. In the event of the disability of the governor, the lieutenant governor shall assume the powers and duties of governor until the disability is removed. The legislature shall provide by law for the succession to the office of governor should the offices of governor and lieutenant governor be vacant, and for the assumption of the powers and duties of governor during the disability of the governor, should the office of lieutenant governor be vacant or the lieutenant governor be disabled. When the office of secretary of state or attorney general is vacant, the governor shall fill the vacancy by appointment for the remainder of the term. If the secretary of state or attorney general is disabled, the governor shall name a person to assume the powers and duties of the office until the disability is removed. The procedure for determining disability and the removal thereof shall be provided by law.

Section 12. Lieutenant Governor

The lieutenant governor shall assist the governor and have such other powers and duties as are prescribed by law.

Section 13. Eliminated by revision.

Section 14. Eliminated by revision.

Section 15. Compensation of Officers

The officers mentioned in this article shall at stated times receive for their services a such compensation as is established by law, which shall not be diminished during their terms of office, unless by general law applicable to all salaried officers of the state. Any person exercising the powers and duties of an office mentioned in this article shall receive the compensation established by law for that office.

Section 16. Eliminated by revision.

Article II: Legislative

Section 1. Legislative Power

The legislative power of this state shall be vested in a house of representatives and senate.

Section 2. Senators and Representatives

The number of representatives and senators shall be regulated by law, but shall not exceed one hundred twenty-five representatives and forty senators. Representatives and senators shall be elected from single-member districts prescribed by law. Representatives shall be elected for two year terms. Senators shall be elected for four year terms. The terms of representatives and senators shall commence on the second Monday of January of the year following election.

Section 3. Compensation of Members of Legislature

The members of the legislature shall receive such compensation as may be provided by law or such compensation as is determined according to law.

Section 4. Qualifications of Members

During the time that any person is a candidate for nomination or election to the legislature and during the term of each legislator, such candidate or legislator shall be and remain a qualified elector who resides in his or her district.

Section 5. Eligibility and Disqualification of Members

No member of congress and no civil officer or employee of the United States or of any department, agency, or instrumentality thereof shall be eligible to be a member of the legislature. Any member of the legislature who accepts any appointment or election contrary to the foregoing shall be disqualified as a member of the legislature.

Section 6. Eliminated by revision.

Section 7. Eliminated by revision.

Section 8. Organization and Sessions

The legislature shall meet in regular session annually commencing on the second Monday in January, and all sessions shall be held at the state capital. The duration of regular sessions held in even-numbered years shall not exceed ninety calendar days. Such sessions may be extended beyond ninety calendar days by an affirmative vote of two-thirds of the members elected to each house. Bills and concurrent resolutions under consideration by the legislature upon adjournment of a regular session held in an odd-numbered year may be considered at the next succeeding regular session held in an even-numbered year, as if there had been no such adjournment.

The legislature shall be organized concurrently with the terms of representatives except that the senate shall remain organized during the terms of senators. The president of the senate shall preside over the senate, and the speaker of the house of representatives shall preside over the house of representatives. A majority of the members then elected (or appointed) and qualified of the house of representatives or the senate shall constitute a quorum of that house. Neither house, without the consent of the other, shall adjourn for more than two days, Sundays excepted. Each house shall elect its presiding officer and determine the rules of its proceedings, except that the two houses may adopt joint rules on certain matters and provide for the manner of change thereof. Each house shall provide for the expulsion or censure of members in appropriate cases. Each house shall be the judge of elections, returns and qualifications of its own members.

Section 9. Vacancies in Legislature

All vacancies occurring in either house shall be filled as provided by law.

Section 10. Journals

Each house shall publish a journal of its proceedings. The affirmative and negative votes upon the final passage of every bill and every concurrent resolution for amendment of this constitution or ratification of an amendment to the Constitution of the United States shall be entered in the journal. Any member of either house may make written protest against any act or resolution, and the same shall be entered in the journal without delay or alteration.

Section 11. Eliminated by revision.

Section 12. Origination by Either house

Bills and concurrent resolutions may originate in either house, but may be amended or rejected by the other.

Section 13. Majority for Passage of Bills

A majority of the members then elected (or appointed) and qualified of each house, voting in the affirmative, shall be necessary to pass any bill. Two-thirds (2/3) of the members then elected (or appointed) and qualified in each house, voting in the affirmative, shall be necessary to ratify any amendment to the Constitution of the United States or to make any application for congress to call a convention for proposing amendments to the Constitution of the United States.

Section 14. Approval of Bills; Vetoes

(a) Within ten days after passage, every bill shall be signed by the presiding officers and presented to the governor. If the governor approves a bill, he shall sign it. If the governor does not approve a bill, the governor shall veto it by returning the bill, with a veto message of the objections, to the house of origin of the bill. Whenever a veto message is so received, the message shall be entered in the journal and in not more than thirty

calendar days (excluding the day received), the house of origin shall reconsider the bill. If two-thirds of the members then elected (or appointed) and qualified shall vote to pass the bill, it shall be sent, with the veto message, to the other house, which shall in not more than thirty calendar days (excluding the day received) also reconsider the bill, and if approved by two-thirds of the members then elected (or appointed) and qualified, it shall become a law, notwithstanding the governor's veto.
If any bill shall not be returned within ten calendar days (excluding the day presented) after it shall have been presented to the governor, it shall become a law in like manner as if it had been signed by the governor.

(b) If any bill presented to the governor contains several items of appropriation of money, one or more of such items may be disapproved by the governor while the other portion of the bill is approved by the governor. In case the governor does so disapprove, a veto message of the governor stating the item or items disapproved, and the reasons therefor, shall be appended to the bill at the time it is signed, and the bill shall be returned with the veto message to the house of origin of the bill. Whenever a veto message is so received, the message shall be entered in the journal and, in not more than thirty calendar days, the house of origin shall reconsider the items of the bill which have been disapproved. If two-thirds of the members then elected (or appointed) and qualified shall vote to approve any item disapproved by the governor, the bill, with the veto message, shall be sent to the other house, which shall in not more than thirty calendar days also reconsider each such item so approved by the house of origin, and if approved by two-thirds of all the members then elected (or appointed) and qualified, any such item shall take effect and become a part of the bill.

Section 15.   Requirements Before Bill Passed

No bill shall be passed on the day that it is introduced, unless in case of emergency declared by two-thirds of the members present in the house where a bill is pending.

Section 16. Subject and Title of Bills; Amendment or Revival of Statutes

No bill shall contain more than one subject, except appropriation bills and bills for revision or codification of statutes. The subject of each bill shall be expressed in its title. No law shall be revived or amended, unless the new act contain the entire act revived or the section or sections amended, and the section or sections so amended shall be repealed. The provisions of this section shall be liberally construed to effectuate the acts of the legislature.

Section 17. Uniform Operation of Laws of a General Nature

All laws of a general nature shall have a uniform operation throughout the state: Provided, The legislature may designate areas in counties that have become urban in character as "urban areas" and enact special laws giving to any one or more of such counties or urban areas such powers of local government and consolidation of local government as the legislature may deem proper.

Section 18. Election or Appointment of Officers; Filling Vacancies

The legislature may provide for the election or appointment of all officers and the filling of all vacancies not otherwise provided for in this constitution.

Section 19. Publication of Acts

No act shall take effect until the enacting bill is published as provided by law.

Section 20. Enacting Clause of Bills; Laws Enacted Only by Bill

The enacting clause of all bills shall be "Be it enacted by the Legislature of the State of Kansas." No law shall be enacted except by bill.

Section 21. Delegation of Powers of Local Legislation and Administration

The legislature may confer powers of local legislation and administration upon political subdivisions.

Section 22. Legislative Immunity

For any speech, written document or debate in either house, the members shall not be questioned elsewhere. No member of the legislature shall be subject to arrest -- except for treason, felony or breach of the peace -- in going to, or returning from, the place of meeting, or during the continuance of the session; neither shall he be subject to the service of any civil process during the session, nor for fifteen days previous to its commencement.

Section 23. Eliminated by revision.

Section 24. Appropriations

No money shall be drawn from the treasury except in pursuance of a specific appropriation made by law.

Section 25. Eliminated by revision.

Section 26. Repealed.

Section 27. Impeachment

The house of representatives shall have the sole power to impeach. All impeachments shall be tried by the senate; and when sitting for that purpose, the senators shall take an oath to do justice according to the law and the evidence. No person shall be convicted without the concurrence of two-thirds of the senators then elected (or appointed) and qualified.

Section 28. Officers Impeachable; Grounds; Punishment

The governor and all other officers under this constitution, shall be removed from office on impeachment for, and conviction of treason, bribery, or other high crimes and misdemeanors.

Section 29. Eliminated by revision.

Section 30. Delegation of Powers to Interstate Bodies

The legislature may confer legislative powers upon interstate bodies, comprised of officers of this state or its political subdivisions acting in conjunction with officers of other jurisdictions, relating to the functions thereof. Any such delegation, and any agreement made thereunder shall be subject to limitation, change or termination by the legislature, unless contained in a compact approved by the congress.

Article III: Judicial

Section 1. Judicial Power; Seals; Rules

The judicial power of this state shall be vested exclusively in one court of justice, which shall be divided into one supreme court, district courts, and such other courts as are provided by law; and all courts of record shall have a seal. The supreme court shall have general administrative authority over all courts in this state.

Section 2. Supreme Court

The supreme court shall consist of not less than seven justices who shall be selected as provided by this article. All cases shall be heard with not fewer than four justices sitting and the concurrence of a majority of the justices sitting and of not fewer than four justices shall be necessary for a decision. The term of office of the justices shall be six years except as hereinafter provided. The justice who is senior in continuous term of service shall be chief justice, and in case two or more have continuously served during the same period the senior in age of these shall be chief justice. A justice may decline or resign from the office of chief justice without resigning from the court. Upon such declination or resignation, the justice who is next senior in continuous term of service shall become chief justice. During incapacity of a chief justice, the duties, powers and emoluments of the office shall devolve upon the justice who is next senior in continuous service.

Section 3. Jurisdiction and Terms

The supreme court shall have original jurisdiction in proceedings in quo warranto, mandamus, and habeas corpus; and such appellate jurisdiction as may be provided by law. It shall hold one term each year at the seat of government and such other terms at such places as may be provided by law, and its jurisdiction shall be co-extensive with the state.

Section 4. Reporter; Clerk

There shall be appointed, by the justices of the supreme court, a reporter and clerk of said court, who shall hold their offices two years, and whose duties shall be prescribed by law.

Section 5. Selection of Justices of the Supreme Court

(a) Any vacancy occurring in the office of any justice of the supreme court and any position to be open thereon as a result of enlargement of the court, or the retirement or failure of an incumbent to file his declaration of candidacy to succeed himself as hereinafter required, or failure of a justice to be elected to succeed himself, shall be filled by appointment by the governor of one of three persons possessing the qualifications of office who shall be nominated and whose names shall be submitted to the governor by the supreme court nominating commission established as hereinafter provided.

(b) In event of the failure of the governor to make the appointment within sixty days from the time the names of the nominees are submitted to him, the chief justice of the supreme court shall make the appointment from such nominees.

(c) Each justice of the supreme court appointed pursuant to provisions of subsection (a) of this section shall hold office for an initial term ending on the second Monday in January following the first general election that occurs after the expiration of twelve months in office. Not less than sixty days prior to the holding of the general election next preceding the expiration of his term of office, any justice of the supreme court may file in the office of the secretary of state a declaration of candidacy for election to succeed himself. If a declaration is not so filed, the position held by such justice shall be open from the expiration of his term of office. If such declaration is filed, his name shall be submitted at the next general election to the electors of the state on a separate judicial ballot, without party designation, reading substantially as follows:

"Shall

_____

(Here insert name of justice.)

_____

(Here insert the title of the court.)

be retained in office?"

If a majority of those voting on the question vote against retaining him in office, the position or office which he holds shall be open upon the expiration of his term of office; otherwise he shall, unless removed for cause, remain in office for the regular term of six years from the second Monday in January following such election. At the expiration of each term he shall, unless by law he is compelled to retire, be eligible for retention in office by election in the manner prescribed in this section.

(d) A nonpartisan nominating commission whose duty it shall be to nominate and submit to the governor the names of persons for appointment to fill vacancies in the office of any justice of the supreme court is hereby established, and shall be known as the "supreme court nominating commission." Said commission shall be organized as hereinafter provided.

(e) The supreme court nominating commission shall be composed as follows: One member, who shall be chairman, chosen from among their number by the members of the bar who are residents of and licensed in Kansas; one member from each congressional district chosen from among their number by the resident members of the bar in each such district; and one member, who is not a lawyer, from each congressional district, appointed by the governor from among the residents of each such district.

(f) The terms of office, the procedure for selection and certification of the members of the commission and provision for their compensation or expenses shall be as provided by the legislature.

(g) No member of the supreme court nominating commission shall, while he is a member, hold any other public office by appointment or any official position in a political party or for six months thereafter be eligible for nomination for the office of justice of the supreme court. The commission may act only by the concurrence of a majority of its members.

Section 6. District Courts

(a) The state shall be divided into judicial districts as provided by law. Each judicial district shall have at least one district judge. The term of office of each judge of the district court shall be four years. District court shall be held at such times and places as may be provided by law. The district judges shall be elected by the electors of the respective judicial districts unless the electors of a judicial district have adopted and not subsequently rejected a method of nonpartisan selection. The legislature shall provide a method of nonpartisan selection of district judges and for the manner of submission and resubmission thereof to the electors of a judicial district. A nonpartisan method of selection of district judges may be adopted, and once adopted may be rejected, only by a majority of electors of a judicial district voting on the question at an election in which the proposition is submitted. Whenever a vacancy occurs in the office of district judge, it shall be filled by appointment by the governor until the next general election that occurs more than thirty days after such vacancy, or as may be provided by such nonpartisan method of selection.

(b) The district courts shall have such jurisdiction in their respective districts as may be provided by law.

(c) The legislature shall provide for clerks of the district courts.

(d) Provision may be made by law for judges pro tem of the district court.

(e) The supreme court or any justice thereof shall have the power to assign judges of district courts temporarily to other districts.

(f) The supreme court may assign a district judge to serve temporarily on the supreme court.

Section 7.   Qualifications of Justices and Judges

Justices of the supreme court and judges of the district courts shall be at least thirty years of age and shall be duly authorized by the supreme court of Kansas to practice law in the courts of this state and shall possess such other qualifications as may be prescribed by law.

Section 8.   Prohibition of Political Activity by Justices and Certain Judges

No justice of the supreme court who is appointed or retained under the procedure of section 5 of this article, nor any judge of the district court holding office under a nonpartisan method authorized in subsection (a) of section 6 of this article, shall directly or indirectly make any contribution to or hold any office in a political party or organization or take part in any political campaign.

Section 9.   Eliminated by revision.

Section 10.   Eliminated by revision.

Section 11.   Stricken from article.

Section 12. Extension of Terms Until Successor Qualified

All judicial officers shall hold their offices until their successors shall have qualified.

Section 13. Compensation of Justices and Judges; Certain Limitation

The justices of the supreme court and judges of the district courts shall receive for their services such compensation as may be provided by law, which shall not be diminished during their terms of office, unless by general law applicable to all salaried officers of the state. Such justices or judges shall receive no fees or perquisites nor hold any other office of profit or trust under the authority of the state, or the United States except as may be provided by law, or practice law during their continuance in office.

Section 14. Eliminated by revision.

Section 15. Removal of Justices and Judges

Justices of the supreme court may be removed from office by impeachment and conviction as prescribed in article 2 of this constitution. In addition to removal by impeachment and conviction, justices may be retired after appropriate hearing, upon certification to the governor, by the supreme court nominating commission that such justice is so incapacitated as to be unable to perform adequately his duties. Other judges shall be subject to retirement for incapacity, and to discipline, suspension and removal for cause by the supreme court after appropriate hearing.

Section 16. Savings Clause

Nothing contained in this amendment to the constitution shall:

(a) Shorten the term of office or abolish the office of any justice of the supreme court, any judge of the district court, or any other judge of any other court who is holding office at the time this amendment becomes effective, or who is holding office at the time of adoption, rejection, or resubmission of a nonpartisan method of selection of district judges as provided in subsection (a) of section 6 hereof, and all such justices and judges shall hold their respective offices for the terms for which elected or appointed unless sooner removed in the manner provided by law;

(b) repeal any statute of this state relating to the supreme court, the supreme court nominating commission, district courts, or any other court, or relating to the justices or judges of such courts, and such statutes shall remain in force and effect until amended or repealed by the legislature.

Section 17. Eliminated by revision.

Section 18. Stricken from article.

Section 19. Eliminated by revision.

Section 20. Eliminated by revision.

Article IV: Elections

Section 1. Mode of Voting

All elections by the people shall be by ballot or voting device, or both, as the legislature shall by law provide.

Section 2. General Elections.

General elections shall be held biennially on the Tuesday succeeding the first Monday in November in even-numbered years. Not less than three county commissioners shall be elected in each organized county in the state, as provided by law.

Section 3. Recall of Elected Officials

All elected public officials in the state, except judicial officers, shall be subject to recall by voters of the state or political subdivision from which elected. Procedures and grounds for recall shall be prescribed by law.

Section 4. Eliminated by revision.

Section 5. Eliminated by revision.

Article V: Suffrage

Section 1. Qualifications of Electors

Every citizen of the United States who has attained the age of eighteen years and who resides in the voting area in which he or she seeks to vote shall be deemed a qualified elector. Laws of this state relating to voting for presidential electors and candidates for the office of president and vice-president of the United States shall comply with the laws of the United States relating thereto. A citizen of the United States, who is otherwise qualified to vote in Kansas for presidential electors and candidates for the offices of president and vice-president of the United States may vote for such officers either in person or by absentee ballot notwithstanding the fact that such person may have become a nonresident of this state if his or her removal from this state occurs during a period in accordance with federal law next preceding such election. A person who is otherwise a qualified elector may vote in the voting area of his or her former residence either in person or by absentee ballot notwithstanding the fact that such person may have become a nonresident of such voting area during a period prescribed by law next preceding the election at which he or she seeks to vote, if his new residence is in another voting area in the state of Kansas.

Section 2. Disqualification to Vote

The legislature may, by law, exclude persons from voting because of commitment to a jail or penal institution. No person convicted of a felony under the laws of any state or of the United States, unless pardoned or restored to his civil rights, shall be qualified to vote.

Section 3. Eliminated by Revision

Section 4. Proof of Right to Vote

The legislature shall provide by law for proper proofs of the right of suffrage.

Section 5. Repealed.

Section 6. Eliminated by revision.

Section 7. Privileges of Electors

Electors, during their attendance at elections, and in going to and returning therefrom, shall be privileged from arrest in all cases except felony or breach of the peace.

Section 8. Eliminated by revision.

Article VI: Education

Section 1. Schools and Related Institutions and Activities

The legislature shall provide for intellectual, educational, vocational and scientific improvement by establishing and maintaining public schools, educational institutions and related activities which may be organized and changed in such manner as may be provided by law.

Section 2. State Board of Education and State Board of Regents

(a) The legislature shall provide for a state board of education which shall have general supervision of public schools, educational institutions and all the educational interests of the state, except educational functions delegated by law to the state board of regents. The state board of education shall perform such other duties as may be provided by law.

(b) The legislature shall provide for a state board of regents and for its control and supervision of public institutions of higher education. Public institutions of higher education shall include universities and colleges granting baccalaureate or postbaccalaureate degrees and such other institutions and educational interests as may be provided by law. The state board of regents shall perform such other duties as may be prescribed by law.

(c) Any municipal university shall be operated, supervised and controlled as provided by law.

Section 3. Members of State Board of Education and State Board of Regents

(a) There shall be ten members of the state board of education with overlapping terms as the legislature may prescribe. The legislature shall make provision for ten member districts, each comprised of four contiguous senatorial districts. The electors of each member district shall elect one person residing in the district as a member of the board. The legislature shall prescribe the manner in which vacancies occurring on the board shall be filled.

(b) The state board of regents shall have nine members with overlapping terms as the legislature may prescribe. Members shall be appointed by the governor, subject to confirmation by the senate. One member shall be appointed from each congressional district with the remaining members appointed at large, however, no two members shall reside in the same county at the time of their appointment. Vacancies occurring on the board shall be filled by appointment by the governor as provided by law.

(c) Subsequent redistricting shall not disqualify any member of either board from service for the remainder of his term. Any member of either board may be removed from office for cause as may be provided by law.

Section 4. Commissioner of Education

The state board of education shall appoint a commissioner of education who shall serve at the pleasure of the board as its executive officer.

Section 5. Local Public Schools

Local public schools under the general supervision of the state board of education shall be maintained, developed and operated by locally elected boards. When authorized by law, such boards may make and carry out agreements for cooperative operation and administration of educational programs under the general supervision of the state board of education, but such agreements shall be subject to limitation, change or termination by the legislature.

Section 6. Finance

(a) The legislature may levy a permanent tax for the use and benefit of state institutions of higher education and apportion among and appropriate the same to the several institutions, which levy, apportionment and appropriation shall continue until changed by statute. Further appropriation and other provision for finance of institutions of higher education may be made by the legislature.

(b) The legislature shall make suitable provision for finance of the educational interests of the state. No tuition shall be charged for attendance at any public school to pupils required by law to attend such school, except such fees or supplemental charges as may be authorized by law. The legislature may authorize the state board of regents to establish tuition, fees and charges at institutions under its supervision.

(c) No religious sect or sects shall control any part of the public educational funds.

Section 7. Savings Clause

(a) All laws in force at the time of the adoption of this amendment and consistent therewith shall remain in full force and effect until amended or repealed by the legislature. All laws inconsistent with this amendment, unless sooner repealed or amended to conform with this amendment, shall remain in full force and effect until July 1, 1969.

(b) Notwithstanding any other provision of the constitution to the contrary, no state superintendent of public instruction or county superintendent of public instruction shall be elected after January 1, 1967.

(c) The state perpetual school fund or any part thereof may be managed and invested as provided by law or all or any part thereof may be appropriated, both as to principal and income, to the support of the public schools supervised by the state board of education.

Section 8. Eliminated by amendment.

Section 9. Eliminated by amendment.

Section 10. Eliminated by amendment.

Article VII: Public Institutions and Welfare

Section 1. Benevolent Institutions

Institutions for the benefit of mentally or physically incapacitated or handicapped persons, and such other benevolent institutions as the public good may require, shall be fostered and supported by the state, subject to such regulations as may be prescribed by law.

Section 2. Eliminated by revision.

Section 3. Eliminated by revision.

Section 4. Aged and Infirm Persons; Financial Aid; State Participation

The respective counties of the state shall provide, as may be prescribed by law, for those inhabitants who, by reason of age, infirmity or other misfortune, may have claims upon the aid of society. The state may participate financially in such aid and supervise and control the administration thereof.

Section 5. Unemployment Compensation; Old-Age Benefits; Taxation

The state may provide by law for unemployment compensation and contributory old-age benefits and may tax employers and employees therefor; and the restrictions and limitations of section 24 of article 2, and section 1 of article 11 of the constitution shall not be construed to limit the authority conferred by this amendment. No direct ad valorem tax shall be laid on real or personal property for such purposes.

Section 6. Tax Levy for Certain Institutions

The legislature may levy a permanent tax for the creation of a building fund for institutions caring for those who are mentally ill, retarded, visually handicapped, with a handicapping hearing loss, tubercular or for children who are dependent, neglected or delinquent and in need of residential institutional care or treatment and for institutions primarily designed to provide vocational rehabilitation for handicapped persons, and the legislature shall apportion among and appropriate the same to the several institutions, which levy, apportionment and appropriation shall continue until changed by statute. Nothing herein contained shall prevent such further appropriation by the legislature as may be deemed necessary from time to time for the needs of said charitable and benevolent institutions. Nothing in this amendment shall repeal any statute of this state enacted prior to this amendment, and any levy, apportionment or appropriation made under authority of this section before its amendment, and any statute making the same, shall remain in full force and effect until amended or repealed by the legislature.

Article VIII: Militia

Section 1. Composition; Exemption

The militia shall be composed of all able-bodied male citizens between the ages of twenty-one and forty-five years, except such as are exempted by the laws of the United States or of this state; but all citizens of any religious denomination whatever who from scruples of conscience may be adverse to bearing arms shall be exempted therefrom, upon such conditions as may be prescribed by law.

Section 2. Organization

The legislature shall provide for organizing, equipping and disciplining the militia in such manner as it shall deem expedient, not incompatible with the laws of the United States.

Section 3. Officers

Officers of the militia shall be elected or appointed, and commissioned in such manner as may be provided by law.

Section 4. Commander in Chief

The governor shall be commander in chief, and shall have power to call out the militia to execute the laws, to suppress insurrection, and to repel invasion.

Article IX: County and Township Organization

Section 1. Counties

The legislature shall provide for organizing new counties, locating county seats, and changing county lines; but no county seat shall be changed without the consent of a majority of the electors of the county; nor any county organized, nor the lines of any county changed so as to include an area of less than four hundred and thirty-two square miles.

The legislature shall provide for such county and township officers as may be necessary.

Section 3. Stricken from the constitution.

Section 4. Stricken from the constitution.

Section 5. Removal of Officers

All county and township officers may be removed from office, in such manner and for such cause, as shall be prescribed by law.

Article X: Appointment of the Legislature

Section 1. Reapportionment of Senatorial and Representative Districts

(a) At its regular session in 1989, the legislature shall by law reapportion the state representative districts, the state senatorial districts or both the state representative and senatorial districts upon the basis of the latest census of the inhabitants of the state taken by authority of chapter 61 of the 1987 Session Laws of Kansas. At its regular session in 1992, and at its regular session every tenth year thereafter, the legislature shall by law reapportion the state senatorial districts and representative districts on the basis of the population of the state as established by the most recent census of population taken and published by the United States bureau of the census. Senatorial and representative districts shall be reapportioned upon the basis of the population of the state adjusted:

(1) To exclude nonresident military personnel stationed within the state and nonresident students attending colleges and universities within the state; and

(2) to include military personnel stationed within the state who are residents of the state and students attending colleges and universities within the state who are residents of the state in the district of their permanent residence. Bills reapportioning legislative districts shall be published in the Kansas register immediately upon final passage and shall be effective for the next following election of legislators and thereafter until again reapportioned.

(b) Within 15 days after the publication of an act reapportioning the legislative districts within the time specified in (a), the attorney general shall petition the supreme court of the state to determine the validity thereof. The supreme court, within 30 days from the filing of the petition, shall enter its judgment. Should the supreme court determine that the reapportionment statute is invalid, the legislature shall enact a statute of reapportionment conforming to the judgment of the supreme court within 15 days.

(c) Upon enactment of a reapportionment to conform with a judgment under (b), the attorney general shall apply to the supreme court of the state to determine the validity thereof. The supreme court, within 10 days from the filing of such application, shall enter its judgment. Should the supreme court determine that the reapportionment statute is invalid, the legislature shall again enact a statute reapportioning the legislative districts in compliance with the direction of and conforming to the mandate of the supreme court within 15 days after entry thereof.

(d) Whenever a petition or application is filed under this section, the supreme court, in accordance with its rules, shall permit interested persons to present their views.

(e) A judgment of the supreme court of the state determining a reapportionment to be valid shall be final until the legislative districts are again reapportioned in accordance herewith.

Section 2.   Eliminated by revision.

Section 3.   Repealed.

Article XI: Finance and Taxation

Section 1. System of Taxation; Classification; Exemption

(a) The provisions of this subsection shall govern the assessment and taxation of property on and after January 1, 2013, and each year thereafter. Except as otherwise hereinafter specifically provided, the legislature shall provide for a uniform and equal basis of valuation and rate of taxation of all property subject to taxation. The legislature may provide for the classification and the taxation uniformly as to class of recreational vehicles and watercraft, as defined by the legislature, or may exempt such class from property taxation and impose taxes upon another basis in lieu thereof. The provisions of this subsection shall not be applicable to the taxation of motor vehicles, except as otherwise hereinafter specifically provided, mineral products, money, mortgages, notes and other evidence of debt and grain. Property shall be classified into the following classes for the purpose of assessment and assessed at the percentage of value prescribed therefor:

Class 1 shall consist of real property. Real property shall be further classified into seven subclasses. Such property shall be defined by law for the purpose of sub-classification and assessed uniformly as to subclass at the following percentages of value:

(1) Real property used for residential purposes including multi-family residential real property and real property necessary to accommodate a residential community of mobile or manufactured homes including the real property upon which such homes are located....11 1/2%

(2) Land devoted to agricultural use which shall be valued upon the basis of its agricultural income or agricultural productivity pursuant to section 12 of article 11 of the constitution.... 30%

(3) Vacant lots.... 12%

(4) Real property which is owned and operated by a not-for-profit organization not subject to federal income taxation pursuant to section 501 of the federal internal revenue code, and which is included in this subclass by law....12%

(5) Public utility real property, except railroad real property which shall be assessed at the average rate that all other commercial and industrial property is assessed....33%

(6) Real property used for commercial and industrial purposes and buildings and other improvements located upon land devoted to agricultural use....25%

(7) All other urban and rural real property not otherwise specifically sub-classified....30%

Class 2 shall consist of tangible personal property. Such tangible personal property shall be further classified into six subclasses, shall be defined by law for the purpose of sub-classification and assessed uniformly as to subclass at the following percentages of value:

(1) Mobile homes used for residential purposes....11 1/2%

(2) Mineral leasehold interests except oil leasehold interests the average daily production from which is five barrels or less, and natural gas leasehold interests the average daily production from which is 100 mcf or less, which shall be assessed at 25%....30%

(3) Public utility tangible personal property including inventories thereof, except railroad personal property including inventories thereof, which shall be assessed at the average rate all other commercial and industrial property is assessed....33%

(4) All categories of motor vehicles not defined and specifically valued and taxed pursuant to law enacted prior to January 1, 1985....30%

(5) Commercial and industrial machinery and equipment which, if its economic life is seven years or more, shall be valued at its retail cost when new less seven-year straight-line depreciation, or which, if its economic life is less than seven years, shall be valued at its retail cost when new less straight-line depreciation over its economic life, except that, the value so obtained for such property, notwithstanding its economic life and as long as such property is being used, shall not be less than 20% of the retail cost when new of such property....25%

(6) All other tangible personal property not otherwise specifically classified....30%

(b) All property used exclusively for state, county, municipal, literary, educational, scientific, religious, benevolent and charitable purposes, farm machinery and equipment, merchants' and manufacturers' inventories, other than public utility inventories included in subclass (3) of class 2, livestock, and all household goods and personal effects not used for the production of income, shall be exempted from property taxation.

Section 2. Taxation of Incomes

The state shall have power to levy and collect taxes on incomes from whatever source derived, which taxes may be graduated and progressive.

Section 3. Transferred and Renumbered.

Section 4. Revenue for Current Expenses

The legislature shall provide, at each regular session, for raising sufficient revenue to defray the current expenses of the state for two years.

Section 5. Object of Tax

No tax shall be levied except in pursuance of a law, which shall distinctly state the object of the same; to which object only such tax shall be applied.

Section 6. State Debts; Annual Tax; Proceeds

For the purpose of defraying extraordinary expenses and making public improvements, the state may contract public debts; but such debts shall never, in the aggregate, exceed one million dollars, except as hereinafter provided. Every such debt shall be authorized by law for some purpose specified therein, and the vote of a majority of all the members elected to each house, to be taken by the yeas and nays, shall be necessary to the passage of such law; and every such law shall provide for levying an annual tax sufficient to pay the annual interest of such debt, and the principal thereof, when it shall become due; and shall specifically appropriate the proceeds of such taxes to the payment of such principal and interest; and such appropriation shall not be repealed nor the taxes postponed or diminished, until the interest and principal of such debt shall have been wholly paid.

Section 7. Election on Indebtedness

No debt shall be contracted by the state except as herein provided, unless the proposed law for creating such debt shall first be submitted to a direct vote of the electors of the state at some general election; and if such proposed law shall be ratified by a majority of all the votes cast at such general election, then it shall be the duty of the legislature next after such election to enact such law and create such debt, subject to all the provisions and restrictions provided in the preceding section of this article.

Section 8. Borrowing Money by State

The state may borrow money to repel invasion, suppress insurrection, or defend the state in time of war; but the money thus raised, shall be applied exclusively to the object for which the loan was authorized, or to the repayment of the debt thereby created.

Section 9. Internal Improvements; State Highway System; Flood Control; Conservation or Development of Water Resources

The state shall never be a party in carrying on any work of internal improvement except that:

(1) It may adopt, construct, reconstruct and maintain a state system of highways, but no general property tax shall ever be laid nor general obligation bonds issued by the state for such highways;

(2) it may be a party to flood control works and works for the conservation or development of water resources;

(3) it may, for the purpose of stimulating economic development and private sector job creation in all areas of the state, participate in the development of a capital formation system and have a limited role in such system through investment of state funds authorized in accordance with law;

(4) it may be a party to any work of internal improvement, whenever any work of internal improvement not authorized by (1), (2) or (3) is once authorized by a separate bill passed by the affirmative vote of not less than two-thirds of all members then elected (or appointed) and qualified to each house, but no general property tax shall ever be laid nor general obligation bonds be issued by the state therefor; and

(5) it may expend funds received from the federal government for any public purpose in accordance with the federal law authorizing the same.

Section 10. Special Taxes for Highway Purposes

The state shall have power to levy special taxes, for road and highway purposes, on motor vehicles and on motor fuels.

Section 11. Taxation of Incomes; Adoption of Federal Laws by Reference

In enacting any law under section 2 of this article 11, the legislature may at any regular, budget or special session define income by reference to or otherwise adopt by reference all or any part of the laws of the United States as they then exist, and, prospectively, as they may thereafter be amended or enacted, with such exceptions, additions or modifications as the legislature may determine then or thereafter at any such legislative sessions.

Section 12. Assessment and Taxation of Land Devoted to Agricultural Use

Land devoted to agricultural use may be defined by law and valued for ad valorem tax purposes upon the basis of its agricultural income or agricultural productivity, actual or potential, and when so valued such land shall be assessed at the same percent of value and taxed at the same rate as real property subject to the provisions of section 1 of this article. The legislature may, if land devoted to agricultural use changes from such use, provide for the recoupment of a part or all of the difference between the amount of the ad valorem taxes levied upon such land during a part or all of the period in which it was valued in accordance with the provisions of this section and the amount of ad valorem taxes which would have been levied upon such land during such period had it not been in agricultural use and had it been valued, assessed and taxed in accordance with section 1 of this article.

Section 13. Exemption of Property for Economic Development Purposes; Procedure; Limitations

(a) The board of county commissioners of any county or the governing body of any city may, by resolution or ordinance, as the case requires, exempt from all ad valorem taxation all or any portion of the appraised valuation of:

(1) All buildings, together with the land upon which such buildings are located, and all tangible personal property associated therewith used exclusively by a business for the purpose of:

(A) Manufacturing articles of commerce;

(B) conducting research and development; or

(C) storing goods or commodities which are sold or traded in interstate commerce, which commences operations after the date on which this amendment is approved by the electors of this state; or

(2) all buildings, or added improvements to buildings constructed after the date on which this amendment is approved by the electors of this state, together with the land upon which such buildings or added improvements are located, and all tangible personal property purchased after such date and associated therewith, used exclusively for the purpose of:

(A) Manufacturing articles of commerce;

(B) conducting research and development; or

(C) storing goods or commodities which are sold or traded in interstate commerce, which is necessary to facilitate the expansion of any such existing business if, as a result of such expansion, new employment is created.

(b) Any ad valorem tax exemption granted pursuant to subsection (a) shall be in effect for not more than 10 calendar years after the calendar year in which the business commences its operations or the calendar year in which expansion of an existing business is completed, as the case requires.

(c) The legislature may limit or prohibit the application of this section by enactment uniformly applicable to all cities or counties.

(d) The provisions of this section shall not be construed to affect exemptions of property from ad valorem taxation granted by this constitution or by enactment of the legislature, or to affect the authority of the legislature to enact additional exemptions of property from ad valorem taxation found to have a public purpose and promote the general welfare.

Article XII: Corporations

Section 1. Corporate Powers

The legislature shall pass no special act conferring corporate powers. Corporations may be created under general laws; but all such laws may be amended or repealed.

Section 2. Liability of stockholders

Dues from corporations shall be secured by the individual liability of the stockholders to the amount of stock owned by each stockholder, and such other means as shall be provided by law; but such individual liability shall not apply to railroad corporations nor corporations for religious or charitable purposes.

Section 3. Repealed

Section 4. Rights of Way; Eminent Domain

No right of way shall be appropriated to the use of any corporation, until full compensation therefor be first made in money, or secured by a deposit of money, to the owner, irrespective of any benefit from any improvement proposed by such corporation.

Section 5. Cities Powers of Home Rule

(a) The legislature shall provide by general law, applicable to all cities, for the incorporation of cities and the methods by which city boundaries may be altered, cities may be merged or consolidated and cities may be dissolved: Provided, That existing laws on such subjects not applicable to all cities on the effective date of this amendment shall remain in effect until superseded by general law and such existing laws shall not be subject to charter ordinance.

(b) Cities are hereby empowered to determine their local affairs and government including the levying of taxes, excises, fees, charges and other exactions except when and as the levying of any tax, excise, fee, charge or other exaction is limited or prohibited by enactment of the legislature applicable uniformly to all cities of the same class: Provided, That the legislature may establish not to exceed four classes of cities for the purpose of imposing all such limitations or prohibitions. Cities shall exercise such determination by ordinance passed by the governing body with referendums only in such cases as prescribed by the legislature, subject only to enactments of the legislature of statewide concern applicable uniformly to all cities, to other enactments of the legislature applicable uniformly to all cities, to enactments of the legislature applicable uniformly to all cities of the same class limiting or prohibiting the levying of any tax, excise, fee, charge or other exaction and to enactments of the legislature prescribing limits of indebtedness. All enactments relating to cities now in effect or hereafter enacted and as later amended and until repealed shall govern cities except as cities shall exempt themselves by charter ordinances as here in provided for in subsection (c).

(c)(1) Any city may by charter ordinance elect in the manner prescribed in this section that the whole or any part of any enactment of the legislature applying to such city, other than enactments of statewide concern applicable uniformly to all cities, other enactments applicable uniformly to all cities, and enactments prescribing limits of indebtedness, shall not apply to such city.

(2) A charter ordinance is an ordinance which exempts a city from the whole or any part of any enactment of the legislature as referred to in this section and which may provide substitute and additional provisions on the same subject. Such charter ordinance shall be so titled, shall designate specifically the enactment of the legislature or part thereof made inapplicable to such city by the adoption of such ordinance and contain the substitute and additional provisions, if any, and shall require a two-thirds vote of the members-elect of the governing body of such city. Every charter ordinance shall be published once each week for two consecutive weeks in the official city newspaper or, if there is none, in a newspaper of general circulation in the city.

(3) No charter ordinance shall take effect until sixty days after its final publication. If within sixty days of its final publication a petition signed by a number of electors of the city equal to not less than ten percent of the number of electors who voted at the last preceding regular city election shall be filed in the office of the clerk of such city demanding that such ordinance be submitted to a vote of the electors, it shall not take effect until submitted to a referendum and approved by a majority of the electors voting thereon. An election, if called, shall be called within thirty days and held within ninety days after the filing of the petition. The governing body shall pass an ordinance calling the election and fixing the date, which ordinance shall be published once each week for three consecutive weeks in the official city newspaper or, if there be none, in a newspaper of general circulation in the city, and the election shall be conducted as elections for officers and by the officers handling such elections. The proposition shall be: "Shall charter ordinance No. _____, entitled (title of ordinance) take effect?" The governing body may submit any charter ordinance to a referendum without petition by the same publication of the charter ordinance and the same publication of the ordinance calling the election as for ordinances upon petition and such charter ordinance shall then become effective when approved by a majority of the electors voting thereon. Each charter ordinance becoming effective shall be recorded by the clerk in a book maintained for that purpose with a statement of the manner of adoption and a certified copy shall be filed with the secretary of state, who shall keep an index of the same.

(4) Each charter ordinance enacted shall control and prevail over any prior or subsequent act of the governing body of the city and may be repealed or amended only by charter ordinance or by enactments of the legislature applicable to all cities.

(d) Powers and authority granted cities pursuant to this section shall be liberally construed for the purpose of giving to cities the largest measure of self-government.

(e) This amendment shall be effective on and after July 1, 1961.

Section 6. Definition of Corporations; Suits

The term corporations, as used in this article, shall include all associations and joint stock companies having powers and privileges not possessed by individuals or partnerships; and all corporations may sue and be sued in their corporate name.

Article XIII: Banks

Section 1. Banking Laws

No bank shall be established otherwise than under a general banking law, nor be operated otherwise than by a duly organized corporation.

Section 2. State not to be Stockholder

The state shall not be a stockholder in any banking institution, except that any retirement or pension plan authorized pursuant to the laws of this state may be a stockholder in any banking institution.

Section 3. Eliminated by revision.

Section 4. Eliminated by revision.

Section 5. Transferred and renumbered as Section 2 by revision.

Section 6. Eliminated by revision.

Section 7. Eliminated by revision.

Section 8. Eliminated by revision.

Section 9. Eliminated by revision.

Article XIV: Constitutional Amendment and Revision

Section 1. Proposals by Legislature; Approval by Electors

Propositions for the amendment of this constitution may be made by concurrent resolution originating in either house of the legislature, and if two-thirds of all the members elected (or appointed) and qualified of each house shall approve such resolution, the secretary of state shall cause such resolution to be published in the manner provided by law. At the next election for representatives or a special election called by concurrent resolution of the legislature for the purpose of submitting constitutional propositions, such proposition to amend the constitution shall be submitted, both by title and by the amendment as a whole, to the electors for their approval or rejection. The title by which a proposition is submitted shall be specified in the concurrent resolution making the proposition and shall be a brief nontechnical statement expressing the intent or purpose of the proposition and the effect of a vote for and a vote against the proposition. If a majority of the electors voting on any such amendment shall vote for the amendment, the same shall become a part of the constitution. When more than one amendment shall be submitted at the same election, such amendments shall be so submitted as to enable the electors to vote on each amendment separately. One amendment of the constitution may revise any entire article, except the article on general provisions, and in revising any article, the article may be renumbered and all or parts of other articles may be amended, or amended and transferred to the article being revised. Not more than five amendments shall be submitted at the same election.

Section 2. Constitutional Conventions; Approval by Electors

The legislature, by the affirmative vote of two-thirds of all the members elected to each house, may submit the question "Shall there be a convention to amend or revise the constitution of the state of Kansas?" or the question "Shall there be a convention limited to revision of article(s) _____ of the constitution of the state of Kansas?", to the electors at the next election for representatives, and the concurrent resolution providing for such question shall specify in such blank appropriate words and figures to identify the article or articles to be considered by the convention. If a majority of all electors voting on the question shall vote in the affirmative, delegates to such convention shall be elected at the next election for representatives thereafter, unless the legislature shall have provided by law for the election of such delegates at a special election. The electors of each representative district as organized at the time of such election of delegates shall elect as many delegates to the convention as there are representatives from such district. Such delegates shall have the same qualifications as provided by the constitution for members of the legislature and members of the legislature and candidates for membership in the legislature shall be eligible for election as delegates to the convention. The delegates so elected shall convene at the state capital on the first Tuesday in May next following such election or at an earlier date if provided by law.

The convention shall have power to choose its own officers, appoint and remove its employees and fix their compensation, determine its rules, judge the qualifications of its members, and carry on the business of the convention in an orderly manner. Each delegate shall receive such compensation as provided by law. A vacancy in the office of any delegate shall be filled as provided by law.

The convention shall have power to amend or revise all or that part of the constitution indicated by the question voted upon to call the convention, subject to ratification by the electors. No proposed constitution, or amendment or revision of an existing constitution, shall be submitted by the convention to the electors unless it has been available to the delegates in final form at least three days on which the convention is in session, prior to final passage, and receives the assent of a majority of all the delegates. The yeas and nays upon final passage of any proposal, and upon any question upon request of one-tenth of the delegates present, shall be entered in the journal of the convention.

Proposals of the convention shall be submitted to the electors at the first general or special statewide election occurring not less than two months after final action thereon by the convention, and shall take effect in accordance with the provisions thereof in such form and with such notice as is directed by the convention upon receiving the approval of a majority of the qualified electors voting thereon.

Article XV: Miscellaneous

Section 1. Selection of Officers

All officers whose election or appointment is not otherwise provided for, shall be chosen or appointed as may be prescribed by law.

Section 2. Tenure of Office; Merit System in Civil Service

The tenure of any office not herein provided for may be declared by law; when not so declared, such office shall be held during the pleasure of the authority making appointment, but the legislature shall not create any office the tenure of which shall be longer than four years, except that appointments under a merit system in civil service shall not be subject to such limitation. The legislature may make provisions for a merit system under which appointments and promotions in the civil service of this state and all civil divisions thereof, shall be made according to merit and fitness, to be determined, so far as practicable, by examination, which, so far as practicable, shall be competitive.

Section 3. Lotteries

Lotteries and the sale of lottery tickets are forever prohibited.

Section 3A. Regulation, Licensing and Taxation of "bingo" Games Authorized

Notwithstanding the provisions of section 3 of article 15 of the constitution of the state of Kansas the legislature may regulate, license and tax the operation or conduct of games of bingo and instant bingo, as defined by law, by bona fide nonprofit religious, charitable, fraternal, educational and veterans organizations.

Section 3B. Regulation, Licensing and Taxation of Horse and Dog Racing and Parimutuel Wagering Thereon

Notwithstanding the provisions of section 3 of article 15 of the constitution of the state of Kansas, the legislature may permit, regulate, license and tax, at a rate not less than 3% nor more than 6% of all money wagered, the operation or conduct, by bona fide nonprofit organizations, of horse and dog racing and parimutuel wagering thereon in any county in which: (a) A majority of the qualified electors of the county voting thereon approve this proposed amendment; or (b) the qualified electors of the county approve a proposition, by a majority vote of those voting thereon at an election held within the county, to permit such racing and wagering within the boundaries of the county. No off-track betting shall be permitted in connection with horse and dog racing permitted pursuant to this section.

Section 3C. State-Owned and Operated Lottery

Notwithstanding the provisions of section 3 of article 15 of the constitution of the state of Kansas, the legislature may provide for a state-owned and operated lottery, except that such state-owned lottery shall not be operated after June 30, 1990, unless authorized to be operated after such date by a concurrent resolution approved by a majority of all of the members elected (or appointed) and qualified of each house and adopted in the 1990 regular session of the legislature. The state shall whenever possible provide the public information on the odds of winning a prize or prizes in a lottery game.

Section 3D. Regulation of "Raffles" Authorized

Notwithstanding the provisions of section 3 of article 15 of the constitution of the state of Kansas, the legislature may authorize the licensing, conduct and regulation of charitable raffles by nonprofit religious, charitable, fraternal, educational and veterans organizations. A raffle means a game of chance in which each participant buys a ticket or tickets from a nonprofit organization with each ticket providing an equal chance to win a prize and the winner being determined by a random drawing. Such organizations shall not use an electronic gaming machine or vending machine to sell tickets or conduct raffles. No such nonprofit organization shall contract with a professional raffle or other lottery vendor to manage, operate or conduct any raffle. Raffles shall be licensed and regulated by the Kansas department of revenue, office of charitable gaming or successor agency.

Section 4. Repealed.

Section 5. Financial Statements; Publication

An accurate and detailed statement of the receipts and expenditures of the public moneys, and the several amounts paid, to whom, and on what account, shall be published, as prescribed by law.

Section 6. Rights of Women

The legislature shall provide for the protection of the rights of women, in acquiring and possessing property, real, personal and mixed, separate and apart from the husband; and shall also provide for their equal rights in the possession of their children.

Section 7. Salaries Reduced for Neglect of Duty

The legislature may reduce the salaries of officers, who shall neglect the performance of any legal duty.

Section 8. Location of State Capital

The temporary seat of government is hereby located at the city of Topeka, county of Shawnee. The first legislature under this constitution shall provide by law for submitting the question of the permanent location of the capital to a popular vote, and a majority of all the votes cast at some general election shall be necessary for such location.

Section 9. Homestead Exemption

A homestead to the extent of one hundred and sixty acres of farming land, or of one acre within the limits of an incorporated town or city, occupied as a residence by the family of the owner, together with all the improvements on the same, shall be exempted from forced sale under any process of law, and shall not be alienated without the joint consent of husband and wife, when that relation exists; but no property shall be exempt from sale for taxes, or for the payment of obligations contracted for the purchase of said premises, or for the erection of improvements thereon: Provided, That provisions of this section shall not apply to any process of law obtained by virtue of a lien given by the consent of both husband and wife: And provided further, That the legislature by an appropriate act or acts, clearly framed to avoid abuses, may provide that when it is shown the husband or wife while occupying a homestead is adjudged to be insane, the duly appointed guardian of the insane spouse may be authorized to join with the sane spouse in executing a mortgage upon the homestead, renewing or refinancing an encumbrance thereon which is likely to cause its loss, or in executing a lease thereon authorizing the lessee to explore and produce therefrom oil, gas, coal, lead, zinc, or other minerals.

Section 10. Intoxicating Liquors

(a) The legislature may provide for the prohibition of intoxicating liquors in certain areas.

(b) The legislature may regulate, license and tax the manufacture and sale of intoxicating liquors, and may regulate the possession and transportation of intoxicating liquors.

(c) The sale of intoxicating liquor by the individual drink in public places is prohibited, except that the legislature may permit, regulate, license and tax the sale of intoxicating liquor by the drink in public places in a county where the qualified electors of the county approve, by a majority vote of those voting on this proposition, to adopt this proposition, but such sales shall be limited to:

(1) Public places where gross receipts from sales of food for consumption on the premises constitute not less than 30% of the gross receipts from all sales of food and beverages on such premises; or

(2) public places for which a temporary permit has been issued as authorized by law.

At any subsequent general election, the legislature may provide by law for the submission of propositions to qualified electors of counties for:

(1) The prohibition of sales of intoxicating liquor by the individual drink in public places within the county;

(2) the regulation, licensing, taxing and sale of intoxicating liquor by the drink in public places within the county without a requirement that any portion of their gross receipts be derived from the sale of food; or

(3) the regulation, licensing, taxing and sale of intoxicating liquor by the drink in public places within the county which derive not less than 30% of their gross receipts from the sale of food for consumption on the premises. Temporary permits for the sale of intoxicating liquor may be issued in any county in which the regulation, licensing, taxation and sale of intoxicating liquor by the drink in public places is approved pursuant to this section, but no temporary permit shall be issued for the sale of intoxicating liquor by the drink within any county in which the regulation, licensing, taxation and sale of intoxicating liquor by the drink in public places is prohibited.

Section 11.   Repealed.

Section 12. Membership or Non-membership in Labor Organizations

No person shall be denied the opportunity to obtain or retain employment because of membership or nonmembership in any labor organization, nor shall the state or any subdivision thereof, or any individual, corporation, or any kind of association enter into any agreement, written or oral, which excludes any person from employment or continuation of employment because of membership or nonmembership in any labor organization.

Section 13. Continuity of State and Local Governmental Operations

Notwithstanding any general or special provision of this constitution, the legislature, in order to insure continuity of state and local governmental operations in periods of emergency resulting from disasters caused by enemy attack, shall have the power and the immediate duty

(1) to provide for prompt and temporary succession to the powers and duties of public offices, of whatever nature and whether filled by election or appointment, the incumbents of which may become unavailable for carrying on the powers and duties of such offices, and

(2) to adopt such other measures as may be necessary and proper for insuring the continuity of governmental operations including, but not limited to, the financing thereof. In the exercise of the powers hereby conferred the legislature shall in all respects conform to the requirements of this constitution except to the extent that in the judgment of the legislature so to do would be impracticable or would admit of undue delay.

Section 14. Oaths of State Officers

All state officers before entering upon their respective duties shall take and subscribe an oath or affirmation to support the constitution of the United States and the constitution of this state, and faithfully to discharge the duties of their respective offices.

Section 15. Victims Rights

(a) Victims of crime, as defined by law, shall be entitled to certain basic rights, including the right to be informed of and to be present at public hearings, as defined by law, of the criminal justice process, and to be heard at sentencing or at any other time deemed appropriate by the court, to the extent that these rights do not interfere with the constitutional or statutory rights of the accused.

(b) Nothing in this section shall be construed as creating a cause of action for money damages against the state, a county, a municipality, or any of the agencies, instrumentalities, or employees thereof. The legislature may provide for other remedies to ensure adequate enforcement of this section.

(c) Nothing in this section shall be construed to authorize a court to set aside or to void a finding of guilty or not guilty or an acceptance of a plea of guilty or to set aside any sentence imposed or any other final disposition in any criminal case.

Section 16. Marriage

(a) The marriage contract is to be considered in law as a civil contract. Marriage shall be constituted by one man and one woman only. All other marriages are declared to be contrary to the public policy of this state and are void.

(b) No relationship, other than a marriage, shall be recognized by the state as entitling the parties to the rights or incidents of marriage.